The Assassination of Abraham Lincoln

The Assassination of Abraham Lincoln

Dennis Brindell Fradin

Marshall Cavendish
Benchmark

New York

Marshall Cavendish Benchmark
99 White Plains Road
Tarrytown, NY 10591
www.marshallcavendish.us

Library of Congress Cataloging-in-Publication Data

Fradin, Dennis B.
The assassination of Abraham Lincoln / by Dennis Brindell Fradin.
p. cm. — (Turning points of United States history)
Includes bibliographical references and index.
ISBN-13: 978-0-7614-2123-8
ISBN-10: 0-7614-2123-8
1. Lincoln, Abraham, 1809-1865—Assassination—Juvenile literature. I. Title II. Series: Fradin, Dennis B. Turning points of United States history.
E457.5.F69 2006
364.152'4'097309034—dc22
2005016019

Photo Research by Connie Gardner
Cover Photo: Bettmann/CORBIS
Cover: President Abraham Lincoln discusses the end of the Civil War.
Title Page: Reza Estakhrian/STONE/Getty Images

The photographs in this book are used by permission and through the courtesy of: *The Granger Collection:* 6, 10, 14, 16, 21, 32; *Getty Images:* Kean
Collection, 9; MPI, 18; Hulton Archive, 22; Time/Life Pictures/Stringer, 24; *The New York Public Library:* Art Resource, 12, 31, 35; *Corbis:* 19, 26, 28, 37;
Bettmann, 20, 38; Richard T. Nowitz, 27; Medford Historical Society Collection, 39; *Art Resource:* Edward Owen, 30; Brown Brothers: 34.

Timeline: Hulton Archive/Getty Images.

Editorial Director: Michelle Bisson
Art Director: Anahid Hamparian
Printed in China
1 3 5 6 4 2

Contents

CHAPTER ONE:	"Long Abe"	7
CHAPTER TWO:	Plots Against Our Sixteenth President	17
CHAPTER THREE:	"They Killed My Pa!"	25
CHAPTER FOUR:	Aftermath	33
	Glossary	40
	Timeline	42
	Further Information	44
	Bibliography	46
	Index	47

This 1865 photograph shows the log cabin built in 1830 by the young Abraham Lincoln in Macon County, Illinois.

"Long Abe"

Abraham Lincoln was born in a log cabin near what is now Hodgenville, Kentucky, on February 12, 1809. He and his older sister Sarah were the children of Thomas and Nancy Lincoln.

At the age of seven, Abraham moved with his family to Indiana. He helped his father chop down trees and build a new log cabin. His mother died when Abraham was only nine. His father then remarried. Abraham became very close to his stepmother, Sarah Lincoln, who thought he was very bright and sent him to school. Teachers were scarce, though, and Abraham spent a total of only about a year going on and off to backwoods schools.

He taught himself by reading. He read before and after he did his farm-work, and while eating lunch beneath a tree. Reading helped him become a fine speaker.

By age sixteen, Abraham was tall and skinny, but strong. He earned about a quarter a day working on neighbors' farms and building rail fences. In 1828, he suffered another terrible blow when his sister Sarah died. That same year, a neighbor hired him to transport some goods to New Orleans, Louisiana.

Abraham and the neighbor's son built a flatboat, then set off by river. On the way, they were attacked by a gang but fought them off and completed the more than 1,000-mile (about 1,600-km) journey. Abraham was disturbed to see slaves being bought and sold in New Orleans. He wondered: How could the country permit slavery to continue?

After returning home, Abraham gave the twenty-four dollars he had earned to his father. But the Lincolns had not done well in Indiana, so in 1830 they moved to Illinois, settling near Decatur.

Soon Abraham was ready to set out on his own. At twenty-two he moved to New Salem, Illinois, where he worked in a store. After the store closed in 1832, he had many jobs. He served as New Salem's postmaster, chopped wood for rail fences, and became a **surveyor**—someone who measures land boundaries.

This illustration (circa 1820s) shows the young Abraham Lincoln ferrying passengers across the Ohio River at one of his first jobs. The illustration is taken from the book, *The Life of Abraham Lincoln for Young People*.

A portrait of Abraham Lincoln and his wife and three sons at home.

He finally settled on a law career. Lincoln read law books on his own, as was common at the time. He became a lawyer in 1836, establishing his office in Springfield, Illinois. In 1842 he married Mary Todd. The couple raised four sons—Robert, Eddie, Willie, and Tad—in their Springfield home.

Meanwhile, Lincoln had entered politics. He lost a race for the Illinois **legislature** in 1832, but was victorious two years later. During eight years

Abe Lincoln's Speeches

Abraham Lincoln was noted for his memorable speeches. The following are a few excerpts:

"The ballot is stronger than the bullet." —May 1856 (Bloomington, Illinois)

"A house divided against itself cannot stand. I believe this government cannot endure, permanently half slave and half free."

—June 16, 1858 (Springfield, Illinois)

"Let us have faith that right makes might; and in that faith let us to the end, dare to do our duty as we understand it." —February 27, 1860 (New York City)

"We here highly resolve that these dead shall not have died in vain, that this nation, under God, shall have a new birth of freedom; and that government of the people, by the people, for the people, shall not perish from the earth."

—November 19, 1863 (Gettysburg Address)

"With malice toward none; with charity for all; with firmness in the right, as God gives us to see the right." —March 4, 1865 (Second Inaugural Address)

in the Illinois legislature he opposed slavery, although less firmly than he would later. In 1846 he won a seat in the U.S. House of Representatives. He did not run for reelection in 1848, partly because his stand against the Mexican-American War (1846–1848) was unpopular. He returned to Illinois and seemed to be finished with politics.

The fifth debate between Abraham Lincoln and Stephen Douglas for the Illinois Senate seat, which Douglas won. Two years later, they met again when both campaigned for the presidency, which Lincoln won.

By the 1850s Americans were arguing bitterly over slavery, which the South allowed but the North did not. Lincoln reentered politics as an enemy of slavery, and in 1858 became the Republican **candidate** for a U.S. Senate seat. Stephen A. Douglas defeated him, but the contest made Lincoln famous. Because he was nearly six feet four inches tall, he became known as "Long Abe."

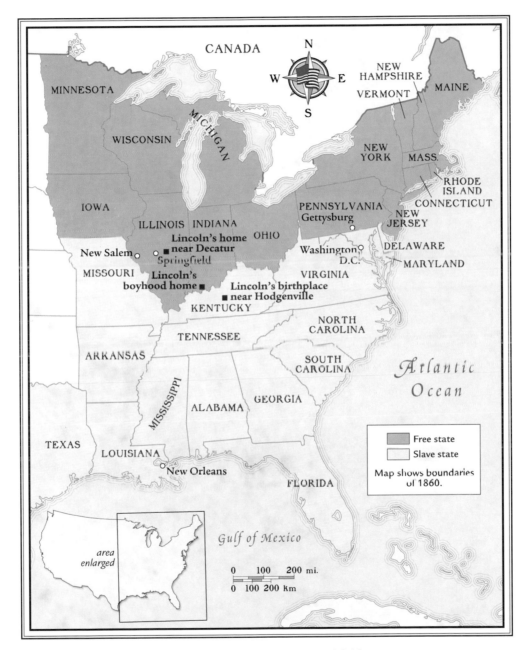

CANADA

MINNESOTA

WISCONSIN

MICHIGAN

NEW HAMPSHIRE

VERMONT

MAINE

NEW YORK

MASS.

IOWA

ILLINOIS INDIANA

Lincoln's home near Decatur ■

New Salem ○

○ Springfield

OHIO

PENNSYLVANIA

Gettysburg ○

RHODE ISLAND

CONNECTICUT

NEW JERSEY

DELAWARE

Washington ○ D.C.

MARYLAND

MISSOURI

Lincoln's boyhood home ■

Lincoln's birthplace near Hodgenville ■

VIRGINIA

KENTUCKY

NORTH CAROLINA

TENNESSEE

ARKANSAS

SOUTH CAROLINA

MISSISSIPPI

ALABAMA

GEORGIA

Atlantic Ocean

TEXAS

LOUISIANA

New Orleans ○

FLORIDA

☐ Free state

☐ Slave state

Map shows boundaries of 1860.

Gulf of Mexico

area enlarged

0   100   200 mi.

0   100 200 km

Slave and Free States in 1860
(Lincoln's homes also shown)

13

This cartoon, published in 1860, shows Republican candidate Abraham Lincoln, once a fence-rail splitter, consoling Democratic candidate Stephen A. Douglas, wearing a feather in his hat on which "KANSAS" is written.

The Republicans chose Lincoln as their candidate for president in 1860. That November he won the election. White Southerners feared that, once in office, Lincoln would act to end slavery. In fact, he had so many enemies in the South that it was believed he would be assassinated (murdered) before he could be sworn in as president.

This 1861 map of the United States shows the seceding states in green.

CHAPTER TWO

Plots Against Our Sixteenth President

In the weeks before Lincoln's **inauguration**, Southern states began to **secede** from the United States. South Carolina went first, on December 20, 1860. Eventually eleven Southern states seceded and joined together as the Confederate States of America.

Meanwhile, the **president-elect** received many death threats. In January 1861, Illinois lawmaker and judge William Joshua Allen described the "gifts" being sent to Lincoln in Springfield: "He has got stacks of preserved fruit and such which he is daily receiving from parts of the South sent as presents. He had several packages opened and examined by medical men who found them to be poisoned."

This engraving by L. Kurz shows Lincoln returning to Springfield, Illinois, after his successful presidential campaign against Stephen A. Douglas in 1860. The home in which he and his family had lived for fifteen years is in the background.

In February 1861 Lincoln said goodbye to friends in Springfield and began a long train trip to Washington, D.C., with many stops planned along the way. A Secret Service to guard the president did not yet exist. But detectives from New York City and Chicago discovered a plot to murder Lincoln in Baltimore, Maryland. Lincoln changed his schedule and passed through Baltimore early, which may have saved him from a band of assassins. He reached Washington safely and took office on March 4 as planned.

Spectators gather at the inauguration of President Abraham Lincoln on the steps of the U.S. Capitol Building in 1861.

The new president faced a giant crisis. On April 12, 1861, the Civil War began. On one side were the Confederate states. Also called the Southern states, they wanted to be a separate country. Opposing them were the Union, or Northern, states. They were led by President Lincoln, who was determined to reunite all the states into one nation and end **slavery**.

President Lincoln speaks to General George B. McClellan at army headquarters at Antietam, October 3, 1862. Antietam was the site of one of the bloodiest battles of the bloodiest war on U.S. land.

Washington, D.C., lay next to Virginia, a Confederate state. Convinced that little could be done to stop an assassin, President Lincoln went about his business with little concern for his safety. He and Tad took walks through the nation's **capital**, with the president stopping to buy his son gingerbread or toys. Often Lincoln traveled alone on horseback to the Soldiers' Home, his family's summer residence, three miles from the White House. Lincoln also made an easy target during frequent visits to the theater and when he relaxed by playing an early version of baseball outside the White House.

He had many close calls. There was a plot to blow up the White House, and several plots to capture the president during his rides to and from the Soldiers' Home. Once as he approached the Soldiers' Home, someone fired a rifle his way. But the bullet missed, and Lincoln's only complaint was that he lost his hat getting away.

A page from Abraham Lincoln's Emancipation Proclamation, 1863.

On November 19, 1863, Lincoln made his famous Gettysburg Address speech at the dedication of the Gettysburg National Cemetery.

On January 1, 1863, as the war raged on, Lincoln issued the **Emancipation** Proclamation, which led to the end of slavery. That November, at the site of a huge battle, Lincoln gave his famous Gettysburg Address, declaring that the war was being fought so that "government of the people, by the people, for the people, shall not perish from the earth." Lincoln was reelected as president in 1864. The next year, on April 9, the Union finally won the Civil War. More than 600,000 soldiers had died, but the Union victory meant that the nation would be reunited and the remaining slaves would be freed.

Lincoln's Last Speech

On the evening of April 11, 1865, Abraham Lincoln made his last public speech, talking to several hundred people gathered on the White House lawn. The president spoke about accepting the Southern states back into the Union and about granting the vote to the former slaves. One of the listeners, John Wilkes Booth, turned to his friend Lewis Paine and said: "That will be the last speech he will ever make."

This photograph shows the outside of Ford's Theatre.

CHAPTER THREE

"They Killed My Pa!"

As he and his wife rode by carriage through Washington on April 14, 1865—Good Friday—President Lincoln was a happy man. Noticing this, Mary Lincoln said: "Dear husband, you almost startle me by your cheerfulness."

"And well I may feel so, Mary," the president replied. "The war has come to a close."

That evening the Lincolns were going to see *Our American Cousin* at Ford's Theatre in Washington. The play began at 8:00 p.m., but because of business, the president and his wife arrived late. As the Lincolns took their seats in the flag-draped presidential box, the crowd cheered. Then the play, which was a comedy, continued.

Lincoln Visits Ford's Theatre

During his more than four years as president, Abraham Lincoln went to Ford's Theatre at least thirteen times before the fateful night of April 14, 1865. On one of those theater visits President Lincoln saw John Wilkes Booth appear in a play entitled *The Marble Heart*.

A portrait of John Wilkes Booth.

The people in the theater included a twenty-six-year-old actor, John Wilkes Booth. Although he was not in the play that night, Booth had often performed at Ford's, so his presence was not unusual. But as he headed toward the presidential box, Booth carried with him a deadly combination a gun in his pocket and hatred in his heart. Booth, who had been born near Bel Air, Maryland, in 1838, despised Lincoln for defeating the South and freeing the slaves. He and some friends had hatched a plot, with Booth playing the leading role.

Abraham Lincoln's booth at Ford's Theatre.

The assassination of President Lincoln by John Wilkes Booth is pictured in this lithograph by an unknown artist.

At 10:20 p.m. Booth approached the unguarded president, who was enjoying the play from a rocking chair. Just as the audience let out a burst of laughter, Booth, no more than two feet away, fired a bullet into the president's head. As the president slumped over and Mary Lincoln screamed, the laughter stopped. Booth leaped from the presidential box onto the stage, breaking a leg, yet triumphantly shouting "Sic semper tyrannis!" which means "Thus always to tyrants!" in Latin. Booth then went out into an alley, mounted a horse, and galloped away.

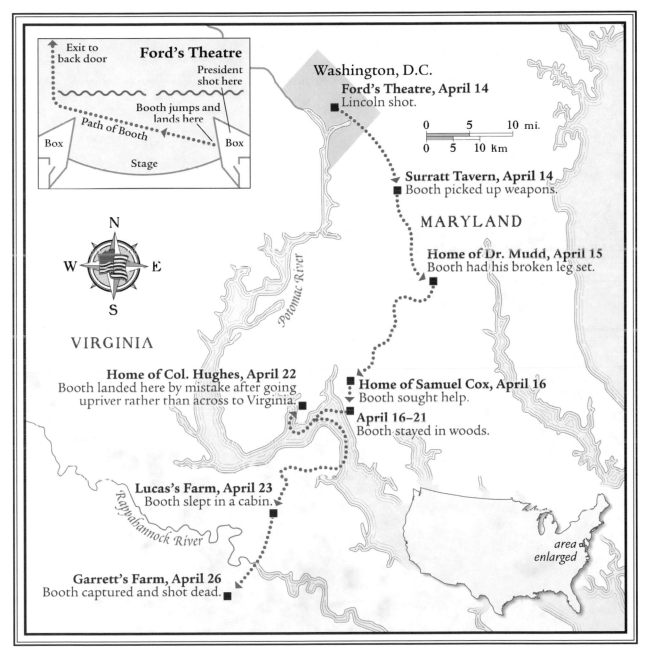

Ford's Theatre

Exit to back door

President shot here

Booth jumps and lands here

Path of Booth

Box

Box

Stage

N W E S

Washington, D.C.
Ford's Theatre, April 14
Lincoln shot.

0   5   10 mi.
0   5   10 km

Surratt Tavern, April 14
Booth picked up weapons.

MARYLAND

Potomac River

Home of Dr. Mudd, April 15
Booth had his broken leg set.

VIRGINIA

Home of Col. Hughes, April 22
Booth landed here by mistake after going upriver rather than across to Virginia.

Home of Samuel Cox, April 16
Booth sought help.

April 16–21
Booth stayed in woods.

Lucas's Farm, April 23
Booth slept in a cabin.

Rappahannock River

area enlarged

Garrett's Farm, April 26
Booth captured and shot dead.

The Escape Route of John Wilkes Booth

The severely wounded president was carried to a house across the street and placed in a bed. It was apparent to the doctors that the president, who had been shot in the brain, would not survive. All they could do was make his last hours comfortable.

Booth had assigned **accomplices** to kill two other Washington leaders that same night. George Atzerodt was supposed to murder Vice President Andrew Johnson in his room at the Kirkwood Hotel, but Atzerodt became frightened and did not carry through the deed. However, Lewis Paine forced his way into the home of Secretary of State William H. Seward and stabbed him repeatedly. Seward was severely injured, but fortunately survived.

The diary of John Wilkes Booth is left open to the day of the assassination. It is on display at Ford's Theatre, in Washington, D.C.

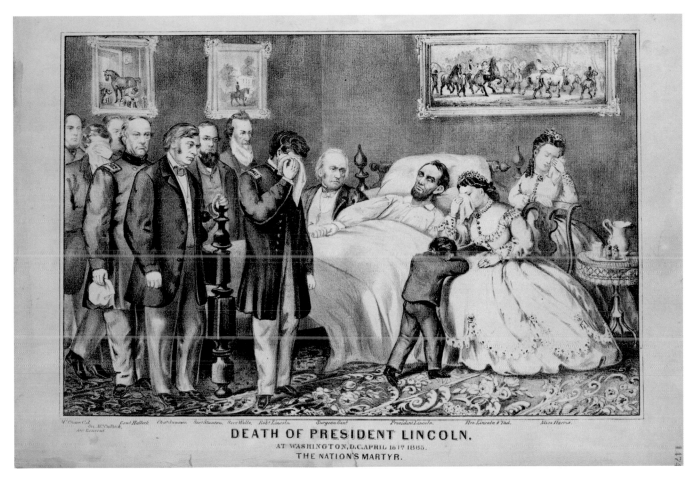

DEATH OF PRESIDENT LINCOLN.
AT WASHINGTON, D.C. APRIL 16TH 1865.
THE NATION'S MARTYR.

This lithograph shows the death of President Lincoln on April 15, 1865.

President Lincoln did not. At 7:22 on the morning of April 15, 1865, the president stopped breathing. After Lincoln died, Secretary of War Edwin Stanton somberly said: "Now he belongs to the ages." When Tad Lincoln learned what had happened, he cried, "They killed my pa! They killed my pa!"

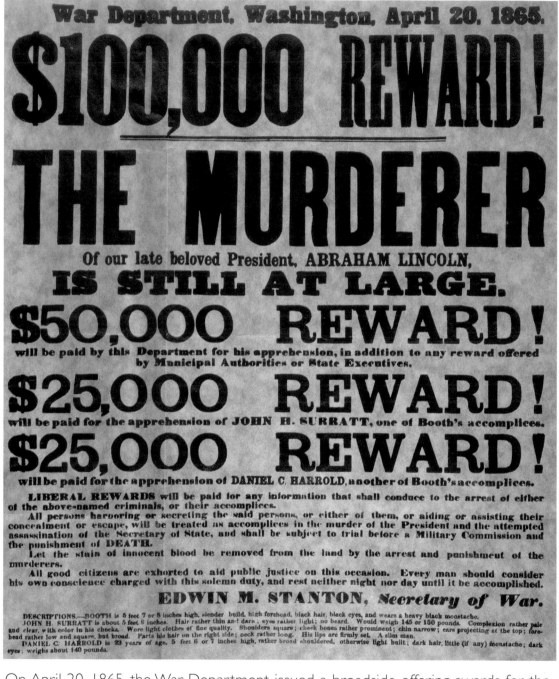

On April 20, 1865, the War Department issued a broadside offering awards for the arrest of John Wilkes Booth and his conspirators in the death of President Lincoln.

CHAPTER FOUR

Aftermath

A service for the president was held in the White House on April 19. Then began a sad 1,600-mile (2,575-km) journey back to Illinois, where Mary Todd Lincoln wanted her husband buried. Along the way, the train bearing the president's body made many stops so that Americans could say goodbye to the man they had called "Long Abe," "Honest Abe," and "Father Abraham." More than 8 million Americans either viewed the president's remains during the stops or gathered near the tracks to see the train pass. By the time Lincoln was laid to rest in Springfield on May 4, nearly a quarter of the country's 35 million people had paid him their respects.

Many thousands of mourners attended President Lincoln's funeral march.

Meanwhile, authorities pursued the people believed to have taken part in the **conspiracy**. **Cavalry** troops (soldiers on horseback) tracked John Wilkes Booth to a barn near Bowling Green, Virginia. The barn was set ablaze and Booth was shot by a soldier. He died on the morning of April 26.

Eight accused conspirators were arrested, tried by a military commission, and given harsh sentences. On July 7, 1865, four of them were hanged: George Atzerodt for planning to murder Vice President Johnson, Lewis Paine for attacking Secretary of State Seward, David Herold for helping Booth escape after he killed the president, and Mary Surratt for aiding the other conspirators. Four others were sentenced to prison: Samuel Arnold and Michael O'Laughlin for plotting with Booth, Dr. Samuel Mudd for setting Booth's broken leg and helping him flee, and Ford's Theatre stagehand Edman Spangler, also charged with helping Booth escape. To this day, some people

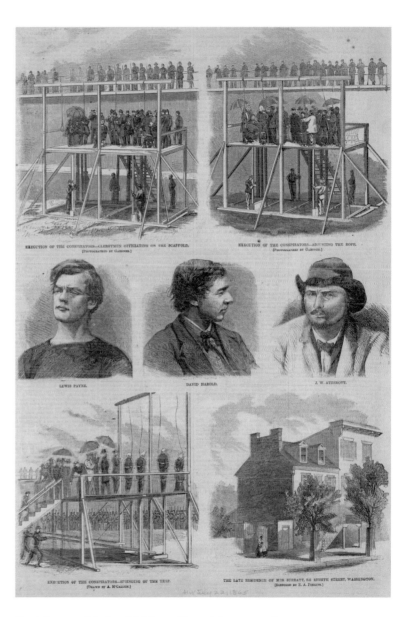

Etchings of John Wilkes Booth's conspirators at their execution.

A Death Predicted

It was said that not long before it happened, Abraham Lincoln had a dream about his own murder. The dream story has often been told to suggest that Lincoln gazed into the future, but a more logical explanation is that he knew he was targeted for assassination.

insist that several of the accused, including Mudd and Surratt, were convicted without proper **evidence** because the government was intent on revenge.

The Lincoln **assassination** was a blow to the United States in many ways. The country had lost its leader at a critical time. Had he lived, President Lincoln might have accomplished the difficult task of bringing the Southern states back into the nation while **guaranteeing** the rights of the former slaves.

As it was, things turned out poorly. During a period called **Reconstruction**, the North stationed soldiers in the South and treated the region like a conquered territory. Although Reconstruction ended in 1877, **friction** between North and South continued for **decades**. Besides, the former slaves were not protected. In 1865 to 1866, whites murdered five thousand black Southerners.

The capture and death of John Wilkes Booth. A cutaway shows him inside the Virginia barn where he hid after he murdered President Lincoln. Federal soldiers set fire to the barn and shot at Booth through the wall.

To make matters worse, the new president, Andrew Johnson, was unpopular. He was **impeached** in 1868 and came within one vote of being removed from office.

Lincoln's murder also began a disturbing trend. Previously, no prominent American had been assassinated. Since then, three presidents have been murdered—James A. Garfield in 1881, William McKinley in 1901, and John F. Kennedy in 1963—and there have also been several unsuccessful attempts on presidents' lives. In addition, other American leaders have been assassinated, including Dr. Martin Luther King Jr. and Senator Robert F. Kennedy, both in 1968.

The assassination of President James Garfield in 1882 is shown here.

The United States created the Secret Service in 1865. At first, its job was to combat the **counterfeiting** of money. Only after President McKinley's assassination in 1901 was the Secret Service assigned to guard the president, as it does today.

After William McKinley was assassinated in 1901, the Secret Service was assigned to protect presidents against assassination attempts.

For nearly 150 years, Americans have been **consoled** by one aspect of Lincoln's assassination. At least he lived long enough to guide us through the Civil War and say: "The war has come to a close."

Glossary

accomplices—Helpers in an act of wrongdoing.

assassination—The murder of a public figure, generally by a secret or sudden attack.

candidate—A person who runs for office.

capital—The place where laws for a nation or state are made.

cavalry—Soldiers on horseback.

console—To comfort, especially in a time of sadness.

conspiracy—A secret plan for wrongdoing.

counterfeiting—The making of a fake duplicate product, such as money or an object of art, with the intent of passing it off as real.

decade—A period of ten years.

emancipation—The act of setting free.

evidence—Clues and other items that furnish proof.

friction—Disagreement or argument.

guarantee—To assure or make certain.

impeach—To charge a public official with serious misconduct in office.

inauguration—The ceremonial act of taking office.

legislature—A body of lawmakers.

president-elect—A person who has been elected president but has not yet taken office.

Reconstruction—The period after the Civil War when the Southern states were readmitted to the Union and forced to form new state governments.

secede—To leave or withdraw from a country or organization.

slavery—The practice of owning people.

surveyor—Someone who measures land boundaries.

Timeline

1809—Abraham Lincoln is born on February 12 in Kentucky

1816—Lincolns move to Indiana

1818—Abraham's mother, Nancy Lincoln, dies

1819—Abraham's father, Thomas Lincoln, marries Sarah (Sally) Bush Johnston

1828—Abraham's sister Sarah dies; Abraham makes a trip to New Orleans, Louisiana

1830—Lincolns move to Illinois

1831—Abraham Lincoln settles in New Salem, Illinois

1832—Lincoln runs for a seat in the Illinois legislature, but loses

1834—Lincoln wins a seat in the Illinois legislature

1836—Lincoln becomes a lawyer

1842—Abraham Lincoln and Mary Todd are married; later they will have four sons

1809   *1830*   *1842*

1846—Lincoln is elected to the U.S. House of Representatives

1858—Abraham Lincoln loses a close election for a seat in the U.S. Senate to Stephen A. Douglas

1860—Abraham Lincoln is elected President on November 6

1861—**March 4:** Lincoln takes office as the sixteenth President
April 12: Civil War begins

1863—**January 1:** President Lincoln issues the Emancipation Proclamation
November 19: President Lincoln makes the Gettysburg Address

1864—Lincoln is reelected as President

1865—April 9: Union wins Civil War
April 14: Lincoln is shot by John Wilkes Booth
April 15: President Lincoln dies

2009—Two hundredth anniversary of the birth of Abraham Lincoln

1860   *1865*   *2009*

Further Information

January, Brendan. *The Assassination of Abraham Lincoln*. New York: Children's Press, 1998.

Somerlott, Robert. *The Lincoln Assassination in American History*. Springfield, NJ: Enslow, 1998.

Zeinert, Karen. *The Lincoln Murder Plot*. North Haven, CT: Linnet, 1999.

WEB SITES

Abraham Lincoln and baseball
http://www.baseball-almanac.com/prz_qal.shtml

A Lincoln assassination Web site with numerous links
http://showcase.netins.net/web/creative/lincoln/education/assassin.htm

Information on the Lincoln assassination
http://memory.loc.gov/ammem/alhtml/alrintr.html

Lincoln assassination artifacts
http://www.loc.gov/exhibits/treasures/trm012.html

The trial of the Lincoln conspirators
http://www.law.umkc.edu/faculty/projects/ftrials/lincolnconspiracy/
lincolnconspiracy.html

Various conspiracy theories on the Lincoln assassination
http://home.att.net/~rjnorton/Lincoln74.html

Bibliography

The Oxford Dictionary of Quotations, 2nd ed. London: Oxford University Press, 1953.

Steers, Edward. *Blood on the Moon: The Assassination of Abraham Lincoln.* Lexington: The University Press of Kentucky, 2001.

Tarbell, Ida M. *In the Footsteps of the Lincolns.* New York: Harper, 1924.

Thomas, Benjamin P. *Abraham Lincoln.* New York: Knopf, 1952.

Index

Page numbers in **boldface** are illustrations.

maps
The Escape Route of John Wilkes
    Booth, 29
    Seceding States, 16
    Slave and Free States in 1860, 13

African Americans, 36
    See also slavery
assassination, 30, 37–38, **38**
    See also under Lincoln, Abraham
Atzerodt, George, 30, 35, **35**

Booth, John Wilkes, 23, **26**, 26–28,
    28, **29**, 30, **30**, **32**, 34, 35, **37**
coconspirators, 30, **35**, 35–36

Civil War, **16**, 19, **20**, **22**, 23, 39
    aftermath, 36–37
Confederate States of America, **16**,
    17, 19
    See also Southern states

Douglas, Stephen A., 12, **12**, **14**

Emancipation Proclamation, **21**, 23

Ford's Theatre, **24**, 25–28, **27**, **28**, 30

Garfield, James A., 37, **38**
Gettysburg Address, 11, **22**, 23

Johnson, Andrew, 30, 37

Kennedy, John F., 37
Kennedy, Robert F., 38
King, Martin Luther Jr., 38

Lincoln, Abraham
    appearance, 8, 12, **22**
    assassination attempts, 15, 17,
        18, 20–21, **24**, 25–31, **28**,
        31, 36
    birth, 7
    early career, 8–12, **9**, **14**
    education, 7–8
    family, 7, 8
    funeral, 33, **34**
    homes, **6**, 7, 8, **18**, 21
    leisure activities, 20–21, 26, **27**
    nicknames, 12, 33
    as president, 15–28, **19**, **20**, **22**, 36
    speeches, 11, **22**, 23
    wife and children, 10, **10**, 20, 25,
        28, 31, 33
Lincoln-Douglas debates, 12, **12**, **14**

McKinley, William, 37

Northern states, 12, **13**, 19, 23, 36

Paine, Lewis, 30, 35, **35**

Reconstruction, 36

Secret Service, 18, 39, **39**
Seward, William H., 30
slavery, 8, 12, **13**, 19, **21**, 23, 27, 36
Southern states, 12, 13, 15, 16, 17,
    19, 36
Surratt, Mary, 35, 36

Union, 19, 23
    See also Northern states

About the Author

Dennis Fradin is the author of 150 books, some of them written with his wife, Judith Bloom Fradin. Their recent book for Clarion, *The Power of One: Daisy Bates and the Little Rock Nine*, was named a Golden Kite Honor Book. Another of Dennis's recent books is *Let It Begin Here! Lexington & Concord: First Battles of the American Revolution*, published by Walker. The Fradins are currently writing a biography of social worker and anti-war activist Jane Addams for Clarion and a nonfiction book about a slave escape for National Geographic Children's Books. Turning Points in U.S. History is Dennis Fradin's first series for Marshall Cavendish Benchmark. The Fradins have three grown children and three young grandchildren.